What Are the Stations of the Cross?

Have you ever taken a train journey? If so, you know that it makes stops at stations along the way. That's where people can get on and off.

Jesus made a journey from the city of Jerusalem to the hill of Calvary. He carried a heavy cross along the Via Dolorosa, which means "Road of Sadness." Jesus stopped many times before he reached Calvary, where he was crucified. The stops on Jesus' journey are now known as the Stations of the Cross—or the Way of the Cross.

Do you know how the Stations of the Cross began? The early Christians loved going to Jerusalem to see where Jesus actually carried his cross. This helped them to pray and to feel close to Jesus. But as Christianity spread to other countries, most people could not make the long pilgrimage to Jerusalem. Then someone had the idea of making fourteen plaques or pictures of Jesus and the stops he made. These became very popular.

Today on the walls of Catholic churches and chapels all over the world, there are Stations of the Cross. Some churches even have Stations outdoors. Next time you go to your church, take a really good look at the Stations. And perhaps you and your family can plan to make a pilgrimage to a nearby cathedral, monastery, or convent to pray the Stations there!

WALKING WITH JESUS TO CALVARY

Stations of the
CROSS

FOR CHILDREN

BY ANGELA M. BURRIN - ILLUSTRATED BY MARIA CRISTINA LO CASCIO

How to Pray the Stations of the Cross

Praying the Stations of the Cross is a great way to talk to Jesus! While many people like to pray the Stations during Lent, you can pray them at any time. You can go to a church, or you can draw your own pictures and put them around your home or even around your backyard. You can also use this book! You can pray the Stations alone or with your family. Or perhaps you can invite a friend to join you on this special journey. Sometimes you may not have time to pray all the Stations, so choose just a few of them.

If this is the first time you have made the Stations of the Cross, here is a simple way to get you started using this book.

First, read about the night before Jesus died on page 8. Then, turn to the first Station and make the Sign of the Cross. Look at the picture. What is happening to Jesus? Read the description on the opposite page. Stop for a moment and talk to Jesus in your own words. Finish the first Station with the prayer. Then turn the page to the next Station. Perhaps you can sing a verse from a favorite hymn as you begin each Station. Other prayers are included at the end of this book.

The Fourteen Stations of the Cross

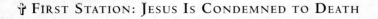

✟ FIRST STATION: JESUS IS CONDEMNED TO DEATH

✟ SECOND STATION: JESUS ACCEPTS HIS CROSS

✟ THIRD STATION: JESUS FALLS THE FIRST TIME

✟ FOURTH STATION: JESUS MEETS HIS MOTHER

✟ FIFTH STATION: SIMON OF CYRENE HELPS JESUS TO CARRY HIS CROSS

✟ SIXTH STATION: VERONICA WIPES JESUS' FACE

✟ SEVENTH STATION: JESUS FALLS THE SECOND TIME

✟ EIGHTH STATION: JESUS SPEAKS TO THE WOMEN OF JERUSALEM

✟ NINTH STATION: JESUS FALLS THE THIRD TIME

✟ TENTH STATION: JESUS IS STRIPPED OF HIS GARMENTS

✟ ELEVENTH STATION: JESUS IS NAILED TO THE CROSS

✟ TWELFTH STATION: JESUS DIES ON THE CROSS

✟ THIRTEENTH STATION: JESUS IS TAKEN DOWN FROM THE CROSS

✟ FOURTEENTH STATION: JESUS IS LAID IN THE TOMB

✟ SOMETIMES THERE IS A FIFTEENTH STATION FOR JESUS' RESURRECTION!

The Night Before Jesus Died

Jesus loves you so much! He is your Savior, King, and friend. That's why he became man over two thousand years ago. While he was on earth, he healed many people—including those who were sick, blind, deaf, unable to walk, or with leprosy. Twice he fed large crowds of hungry people. Jesus taught people how to pray and how to live in a way that would be pleasing to their heavenly Father. He loved children and wanted them to come to him.

But not everyone liked Jesus. He had enemies who wanted to kill him. Jesus knew he was going to die, so after his Last Supper with his disciples, he went to the Garden of Gethsemane. There, on his knees, he prayed, "Father, take this cup from me, but not my will, but yours be done." He prayed so hard that he sweated drops of blood.

Suddenly, soldiers entered the garden. Judas Iscariot, one of Jesus' disciples, was with them. He had betrayed Jesus for the price of thirty pieces of silver. Judas came up and kissed Jesus. That was the sign—now the soldiers knew who Jesus was! The other disciples ran away, and the soldiers took Jesus to Pilate, the Roman governor.

Jesus Is Condemned to Death

It was early on Friday morning when Jesus stood silently in front of Pontus Pilate, his wrists bound together with ropes. Pilate looked at Jesus. He knew Jesus was not guilty of any crime, and he didn't want to crucify him. He didn't know what to do. Then he had an idea.

Pilate came out on the balcony of his palace and said to the crowd, "Today is a special day when I can release a criminal. Who do you want me to release—Jesus, or Barabbas, the murderer?" Pilate hoped they would choose Jesus. But instead the people answered, "Barabbas!" Pilate answered, "Then what shall I do with Jesus?" They shouted, "Crucify him!"

Pilate was shocked. He asked his servant to bring him a bowl of water. In front of the crowd, Pilate washed his hands. This showed that he didn't want to be part of the decision to condemn Jesus to death. Then he sent Jesus away to be whipped and crucified.

Jesus, sometimes I do things that are wrong
just because I want to please my friends.
I want to do things only to please you.
Help me to make good choices.

Jesus Accepts His Cross

Jesus was led into the courtyard of Pilate's palace. Soldiers took off his cloak and tunic and tied him to a pillar. Then they took turns striking Jesus with strips of leather tied to pieces of broken bone. Jesus was in horrible pain as the whip cut into his body.

Some soldiers wanted to make fun of Jesus so they dressed him up like a king! They put a purple cloak on him. One soldier said, "A king needs a crown." They made one from large twisted thorns. They pushed the crown into his head. Another soldier said, "A king needs a royal scepter." So they got a stick and put it in Jesus' right hand. Other soldiers laughed and said, "Hail, King of the Jews."

"It is time to get this man's cross," said a soldier. Two other soldiers dragged it over to Jesus. They placed it in his hands and over his shoulders. As he took the cross, Jesus began to bend over. The cross was so heavy, and he was so weak!

Jesus, I love you. Thank you for accepting the cross.
Whenever I look at a crucifix,
I want to remember how much you love me.

Jesus Falls the First Time

Jesus was led out of Pilate's courtyard, dragging his cross through the narrow, winding streets of Jerusalem. It was about one-third of a mile to Calvary. This was the hill outside the city walls where criminals were nailed to their crosses.

The midmorning air was hot and humid. A crowd of people followed. The rough wood of the cross cut into Jesus' flesh. Sometimes the cross banged against the crown of thorns on Jesus' head.

Suddenly, Jesus lost his balance and fell down. The cross landed on top of him. Some people in the crowd cried out, "Oh, no!" Others began to laugh at him. Jesus stayed on the ground, unable to move. The soldiers were annoyed. They picked up the cross and quickly pulled Jesus to his feet. They wanted their job of taking Jesus to Calvary to be over. Lots of bad language poured out of their mouths. Then Jesus took his cross and began walking again.

Jesus, how tired you must have been, and how much your body must have hurt!
But you didn't complain. Sometimes I complain to my family or friends
when they annoy me or when I'm unhappy about something.
Holy Spirit, when this happens, please remind me to ask for your help.

Jesus Meets His Mother

Jerusalem was filled with people. Some had come there for the Passover feast. Others had come to join the procession to Calvary. Jesus walked along slowly with his heavy cross over his shoulders. In the crowds that followed him was one very special person—Jesus' mother, Mary!

Mary came up to Jesus and reached out her hand to touch him. "My son, I am here with you. I won't leave you alone," she whispered. Jesus' head was down because of the weight of the cross, but he recognized his mother's voice. Jesus stopped walking and looked up at his Mother.

Mary was shocked to see Jesus' face. It was covered with blood and bruises. She felt a stab of pain in her heart. Then she remembered the words of Simeon the prophet when she and Joseph had presented the baby Jesus in the Temple in Jerusalem. Simeon had said to her, "A sword will pierce your heart."

Mary heard one of the soldiers call out to her, "Move back." Another said to Jesus, "Keep walking." Some of Mary's friends comforted her as she left Jesus' side. One of them said, "Mary, we will stay close to you and Jesus."

Mary, I love you. You are my Mother in heaven.
Pray for me. Be with me, just as you were with Jesus.

Simon of Cyrene Helps Jesus to Carry His Cross

Jesus was so exhausted that it was difficult for him to put one foot in front of the other. Someone in the crowd said, "Won't anyone help Jesus? He is struggling to carry his cross."

The soldiers were afraid that Jesus would collapse. One said, "What will we do if Jesus can't finish his walk to Calvary?" Another soldier said, "Get that man. He looks strong." There was a lot of pushing and shoving as the soldiers grabbed a man named Simon of Cyrene. He was a farmer who was visiting Jerusalem for the feast of Passover. Simon looked surprised. But a soldier said, "Quick. Help this man to carry his cross."

Simon obeyed the soldier. He went over to Jesus. He lifted part of the cross onto his strong shoulders. Together Jesus and Simon began walking. That day Simon had to forget about what he had wanted to do. His heavenly Father had another plan—a very special plan. Simon had been chosen to help Jesus, the Savior of the world!

Jesus, Simon of Cyrene was chosen to help you.
I too want to be helpful, both at home and at school.
Every night I want to be able to say,
"Heavenly Father, I helped someone today!"

SIXTH STATION

Veronica Wipes Jesus' Face

Jesus was covered in sweat. Blood continued to trickle down his face from the crown of thorns on his head. Even with Simon of Cyrene's help, Jesus walked very slowly. The soldiers kept kicking his legs and hitting his shoulders with their leather strips.

Suddenly, a woman pushed through the crowd. This took the soldiers by surprise. One yelled, "Get out of our way. We have to get this man to Calvary." But Veronica didn't listen to them. She wanted to help Jesus. When she got to Jesus, he stopped to look at her.

Veronica took off her veil and wiped the blood from Jesus' forehead, eyes, cheeks, and mouth. Veronica was very gentle. She didn't want to hurt him. All she wanted to do was to make him feel better by cleaning his face with her soft veil. Then a miracle happened. When Veronica looked at her veil, she saw the face of Jesus on it! What a precious gift!

Jesus, Veronica comforted you by doing something kind for you.
Help me to do little acts of kindness for others.
It doesn't matter if anyone sees them.
I know that you see everything.

SEVENTH STATION

Jesus Falls a Second Time

As Jesus walked out through the city gates, he was very thirsty, and the heat made it hard for him to breathe. But the soldiers didn't care. One of them said, "Oh, the sun is so hot. Let's just get this job done."

The weight of the cross made the muscles in Jesus' arms and legs ache and cramp. Suddenly, Jesus fell a second time. His mother, Mary, saw him go down. She let out a gasp and said, "Jesus, my son!" But there was nothing she could do to help him. People nearby said, "Look, Jesus has fallen a second time. Will he be able to get up?"

The soldiers were unkind. "Quick! Get up, Jesus!" one of them yelled. A soldier pulled up Jesus by a rope around his waist. Now he could stand up again. Then the soldiers balanced the cross on his shoulders once more. Mary felt another sword piercing her heart.

Jesus, you suffered so much as you carried your cross to Calvary.
When people I love are sick or sad or having a hard time,
I hope I can help them. Holy Spirit, give me
some kind and comforting words to say to them.

EIGHTH STATION

Jesus Speaks to the Women of Jerusalem

Many people in the crowd knew about Jesus. They knew about all the miracles he had done and all the people he had healed. Some women standing together in a group were upset and crying because Jesus was on his way to Calvary to die. One of them said, "Why is this happening to Jesus? He has never done anything wrong." Another said, "Only a few days ago I saw Jesus ride into Jerusalem on a donkey. Everyone was waving palm branches and singing, 'Blessed is he who comes in the name of the Lord! Hosanna in the highest!'"

When Jesus saw the women, he said, "Daughters of Jerusalem, do not weep for me, but weep for yourselves and for your children." With only just a few hours to live, Jesus wasn't thinking about himself. He was thinking about them. Jesus knew they would have hard times ahead, and he wanted them to make good choices that would be pleasing to their heavenly Father.

Jesus, thank you for always thinking about me.
Help me to think about others before I think about myself.
Please open my eyes to the needs and feelings of other people,
especially of my family and friends.

Jesus Falls a Third Time

"Keep moving, Jesus. We are nearly there," one of the soldiers said. Another soldier gave a quick tug on the rope around Jesus' waist, hoping to make him move faster. This made Jesus gasp for breath. He wobbled from side to side, tried to get his balance, and then he fell a third time.

Jesus' mother, Mary, again saw him fall. "Jesus!" she cried out. Some of the onlookers pushed past Mary. "They are beginning to crucify the other two criminals," one said. "Let's get to Calvary quickly."

Mary knew that soon she would have to stand by the foot of the cross, watching her son suffer and die a horrible death. But she also knew that her heavenly Father had a plan. Mary remembered back to the day when the angel had come to tell her that she would have a son. Jesus had been sent into the world for a very special reason. He was going to save people from their sins. He was going to open the gates of heaven!

Jesus, although you were hurting badly, you didn't give up.
You knew you had to die on the cross so that our sins could be forgiven.
Thank you, Jesus, for forgiving me whenever I come to you.
I never want to be separated from you or from
my heavenly Father.

Jesus Is Stripped of His Garments

Dark clouds covered the sky as Jesus picked up his cross and staggered the last few yards to the top of Calvary. Finally, his walk was over.

The soldiers took the cross from Jesus. Simon of Cyrene's job was done, and he stepped back into the crowd. Jesus stood by himself, not saying a word. "Here, Jesus, drink this mug of wine," said one of the soldiers. But when Jesus realized that the wine was mixed with a drug that would make him feel less pain, he refused to drink it. Another soldier said, "Let's takes off his clothes and get him ready for his crucifixion." So they began to roughly pull off his clothes.

"Let's divide up his clothes so that we can each take something home," said one of the soldiers. So they each took a piece of clothing. But Jesus' cloak was made of one piece of material. "Let's not cut it," the soldier said. Then they threw dice to decide who would get Jesus' cloak.

Jesus, as you waited to be crucified,
everything was taken away from you, even your clothing.
There are many people in the world today who have so little.
Help me to find ways to be generous
with what I have.

Jesus Is Nailed to the Cross

The soldiers laid Jesus' cross on the ground near the two criminals, who were already nailed to their crosses. Jesus was so tired that he almost collapsed. "Quick, grab him before he falls!" one of the soldiers said. Then they led him to the cross, turned him around, and pushed him down so that he was laying face-up on the cross.

A soldier stretched out Jesus' arms. With a heavy hammer, he pounded sharp wooden nails through Jesus' hands. He bent Jesus' knees so that his feet would lie flat on the cross and hammered a nail through them. How painful it was for Jesus! Then the soldiers lifted his cross and put it in the ground between the two criminals.

Lifted up high above the crowd, Jesus prayed, "Father, forgive them, for they don't know what they are doing." One criminal said, "If you are the Christ, why don't you save yourself and us?" The other one said, "We are being punished for what we have done. But this man has done nothing wrong. Jesus, remember me when you come into your kingdom." Jesus said to him, "Today you will be with me in paradise."

Jesus, as you hung on the cross, you asked
your Father to forgive those who were hurting you.
Help me to forgive those who upset or hurt me.

Jesus Dies on the Cross

"Jesus of Nazareth, King of the Jews." That's what was written on the sign that was nailed to Jesus' cross. But the chief priest told Pilate, "The sign should say, 'This man said I am King of the Jews.'" Pilate replied, "No. What I have written, I have written."

Mary stood at the foot of Jesus' cross. She wasn't alone. John, Jesus' beloved disciple, was with her. Jesus looked down at his mother and John and said, "Woman, here is your son!" Then to John he said, "Here is your mother!" Later, Mary went to live in John's home.

Someone in the crowd shouted, "If you are the Son of God, come down from the cross." But Jesus didn't answer. A little while later, Jesus cried out, "My God, my God, why have you forgotten me?" Then he said, "I thirst." A soldier soaked a sponge in vinegar, placed it on a stick, and held it up to Jesus' mouth.

After three long hours, Jesus said his last words: "It is finished." His head dropped down, and he took his last breath and died.

Jesus, you suffered so much for me.
Thank you for dying on the cross for my sins.
Jesus, I ask you to come into my heart.
I want you to be my best friend, now and forever!

Jesus Is Taken Down from the Cross

The soldiers were anxious to finish their work. They broke the legs of the two criminals so that they would die more quickly. But when they came to Jesus, one of soldiers said, "There's no need to break his legs. He's already dead." Just to make sure, one of the soldiers took his sword and pierced Jesus' side. Out came blood and water.

It was the eve of the Sabbath. Jewish people were not allowed to do any work on the Sabbath. So Jesus' body had to be taken down from the cross quickly and buried before sundown. Jesus' friend, Joseph from Arimathea, had gotten permission from Pilate to take Jesus' body down from the cross. A ladder was placed up against the cross. The nails were removed from his hands and feet, and Jesus' body was slowly lowered to the ground.

Mary sat on the ground and waited to hold her son. When Jesus' body was placed in her arms, she remembered when she had held him as a newborn baby in the stable at Bethlehem.

Jesus, how sad Mary was as she held you in her arms for the last time.
I will pray for anyone who is sad because a loved one has died.
Please be with them, Jesus,
and comfort them with your love.

FOURTEENTH STATION

Jesus Is Laid in the Tomb

Mary didn't want to let go of Jesus. But Joseph of Arimathea said, "Mary, the sun is setting. We must bury Jesus quickly." Jesus' friend Nicodemus and Joseph gently took Jesus from the arms of his mother. A final sword pierced Mary's heart.

Joseph and Nicodemus carried Jesus' body to a nearby garden. Mary, John, and some of their friends walked behind them, comforting one another. Then Jesus' body was wrapped in strips of fine linen cloth together with some spices. Nicodemus had brought a mixture of myrrh and aloes to anoint the body of Jesus. He said, "There is no time for anointing." Mary Magdalene and some of the other women said, "We can come and anoint Jesus' body after the Sabbath on the first day of the week."

Jesus' body was then carried to a new tomb that belonged to Joseph of Arimathea. Mary watched as her son's body was laid on a flat rock inside the tomb. Finally, it was time to leave. A large stone was rolled against the opening.

Jesus, you have been laid in the tomb.
I want to pray for all those who have died.
If they are still in purgatory,
bring them quickly to heaven so that they can
spend eternity with you.

FIFTEENTH STATION

Jesus Rises from the Dead

On the first day of the week, Mary Magdalene set out for the tomb. When she saw that the stone had been removed, she ran to find Peter and John. "They have taken Jesus out of the tomb," she told them, "and I don't know where they have laid him."

Peter and John ran to the tomb and saw the linen cloths that Jesus had been wrapped in lying there. Mary Magdalene stood outside weeping. As she bent over to look into the tomb, she saw two angels. "Woman, why are you weeping?" they asked. Mary replied, "They have taken Jesus."

Then she heard a voice behind her: "Mary!" She turned around and saw Jesus standing there. Mary said, "Teacher!" Jesus replied, "Do not hold on to me. But go and tell my disciples that I have risen from the dead. I am alive!" Immediately, Mary went and told the disciples, "I have seen Jesus!"

Jesus appeared to his disciples for forty days and then ascended to heaven. But he is alive, and he is with us always!

Jesus, I praise and thank you for your life, your death,
and your resurrection. I want to tell other people how much you love them,
what you did for them on the cross,
and how they can have a special friendship with you!
Jesus, I love you!

Prayer Intentions

I It pleases Jesus when we remember others in our prayers. After you pray a Station, you can lift up someone who needs your prayer. Here are suggestions for groups of people you can pray for after each Station.

☩ My parents, brothers, sisters, and family members.

☩ Children with a serious illness or disability, and their parents.

☩ Those who are looking for jobs.

☩ An end to abortion.

☩ Those who help and protect others (military, fire and sea rescue, and police).

☩ Doctors, nurses, and caregivers.

☩ Those addicted to drugs, alcohol, or involved with gangs.

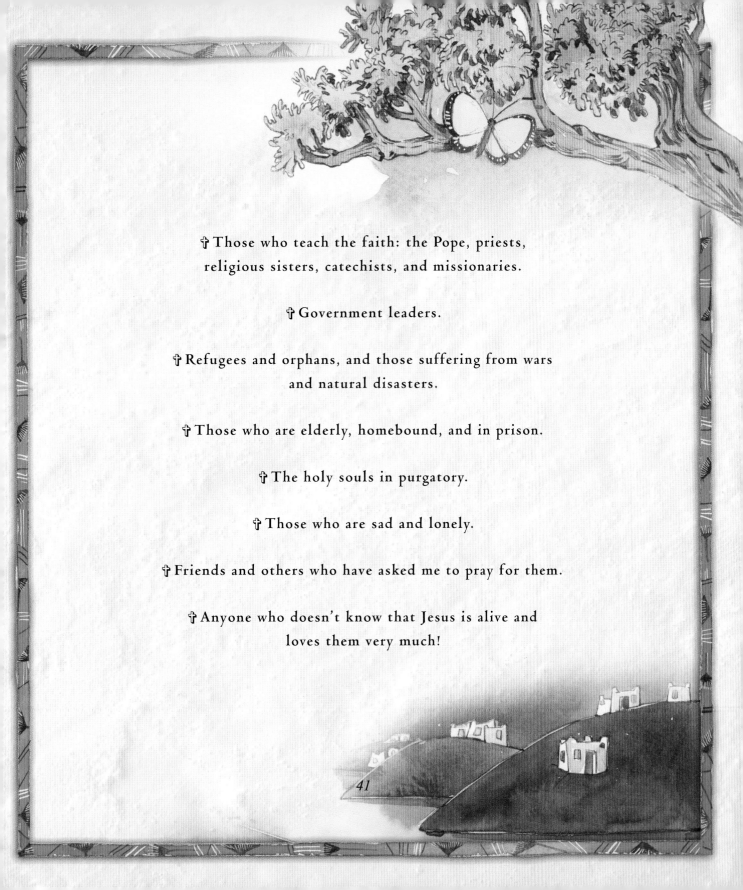

✝ Those who teach the faith: the Pope, priests, religious sisters, catechists, and missionaries.

✝ Government leaders.

✝ Refugees and orphans, and those suffering from wars and natural disasters.

✝ Those who are elderly, homebound, and in prison.

✝ The holy souls in purgatory.

✝ Those who are sad and lonely.

✝ Friends and others who have asked me to pray for them.

✝ Anyone who doesn't know that Jesus is alive and loves them very much!

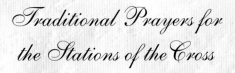

Traditional Prayers for
the Stations of the Cross

The Sign of the Cross:

In the name of the Father, and of the Son,
and of the Holy Spirit.
Amen.

To begin each Station:

We adore you, O Christ, and we praise you.

(kneeling)

Because, by your holy cross,
you have redeemed the world.

(standing)

To end each Station:

I love you, Jesus, whom I love above all things.
I repent with my whole heart of having offended you.
Never permit me to separate myself from you again.
Grant that I may love you always,
and then do with me what you will.

**Then pray
an Our Father,
a Hail Mary,
and a Glory Be.**

Our Father

*Our Father, who art in heaven,
hallowed be thy name;
thy kingdom come;
thy will be done
on earth as it is in heaven.
Give us this day our daily bread;
and forgive us our trespasses
as we forgive those who trespass against us;
and lead us not into temptation
but deliver us from evil.
Amen.*

Hail Mary

Hail Mary, full of grace,
The Lord is with you.
Blessed are you among women,
And blessed is the fruit of your womb, Jesus.
Holy Mary, Mother of God,
pray for us sinners,
now and at the hour of our death.
Amen.

The Glory Be

Glory be to the Father,
and to the Son,
and to the Holy Spirit.
As it was in the beginning,
is now, and ever shall be,
world without end. Amen.

Published in 2014 in the U.S. and Canada by
The Word Among Us Press
Frederick, Maryland
www.wau.org
ISBN: 978-1-59325-245-8

Copyright © 2014 Anno Domini Publishing
www.ad-publishing.com
Text copyright © 2014 Angela M. Burrin
Illustrations copyright © 2014 Maria Cristina Lo Cascio

Publishing Director: Annette Reynolds
Art Director: Gerald Rogers
Pre-production: Krystyna Kowalska Hewitt
Production: John Laister

Printed and bound in Malaysia
August 2013